The Underground Railroad

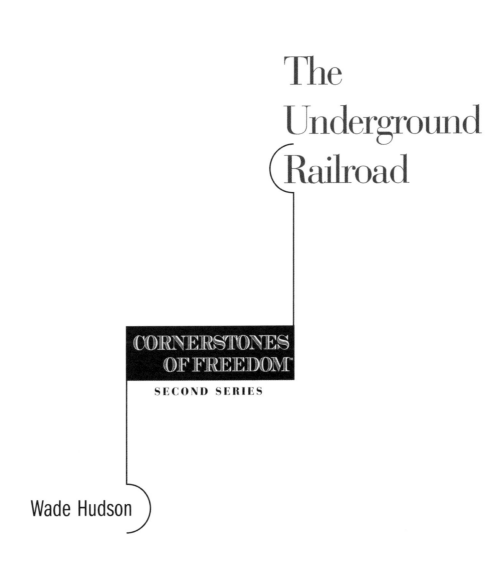

CORNERSTONES OF FREEDOM
SECOND SERIES

Wade Hudson

Children's Press®
A Division of Scholastic Inc.
New York • Toronto • London • Auckland • Sydney
Mexico City • New Delhi • Hong Kong
Danbury, Connecticut

Photographs © 2005: Bridgeman Art Library International Ltd.,
London/New York: 5 (British Library, London, UK); Corbis Images: cover
bottom, 6, 7, 19, 21 top, 27, 33, 37, 44 bottom, 44 top left (Bettmann), 38,
39 (Buxton Historic Site and Museum/Reuters), 20 (Historical Picture
Archive), 23 (Layne Kennedy), cover top, 14 (Francis G. Mayer), 4 (Lee
Snider), 9, 10, 40, 41; Levi Coffin House Association, Fountain City, IN:
25; Library of Congress via SODA: 11, 45 top right; Mary Evans Picture
Library: 18; National Geographic Image Collection: 17; National Park
Service/National Historic Landmarks Collection: 26; New York Public
Library Picture Collection via SODA: 15 top; Collection of the New-York
Historical Society: 31 (#69311); North Wind Picture Archives: 8, 12, 13,
15 bottom, 28, 29, 32, 35, 45 top left, 45 bottom; psihoyos.com/Louie
Psihoyos: 22; SODA/James McMahon/Classroom Magazines: 34; Stock
Montage, Inc.: 24; Superstock, Inc.: 3, 16, 21 bottom, 30, 44 top right.

Library of Congress Cataloging-in-Publication Data
Hudson, Wade.
  The Underground Railroad / Wade Hudson.
    p. cm. — (Cornerstones of freedom. Second series)
Includes bibliographical references and index.
  ISBN 0-516-23630-X
  1. Underground railroad—Juvenile literature. 2. Fugitive slaves—
United States—History—19th century—Juvenile literature. 3. Antislav-
ery movements—United States—History—19th century—Juvenile
literature. I. Title. II. Series.
E450.H87 2005
973.7'115—dc22

                                                        2004010670

1 2 3 4 5 6 7 8 9 10 R 14 13 12 11 10 09 08 07 06 05

THE YEAR WAS 1831. IN the southern state of Kentucky, a slave named Tice Davids had had enough. He decided it was time to try and find his way to freedom in the North. Davids escaped and made his way to the Ohio River. His master followed, trying to recapture his runaway slave.

Sisters Elizabeth and Abigail Goodwin helped many slaves to "disappear" on the Underground Railroad. Their home in New Jersey was used as a safe house for many years.

Standing on the banks of the river, Davids realized he would have to swim across if he was to make his escape. On the other side was the free state of Ohio. Davids plunged into the river. From a distance, his master saw the runaway slave swimming against the current. The master found a boat and took off after his valuable property.

He reached the Ohio shore just minutes after he saw Davids do so. But the escaping slave had disappeared. The master searched and searched, but there was no trace of Davids. He finally gave up and muttered that his slave must have escaped on "an underground road."

This story about the runaway slave escaping on an underground road spread. Perhaps because of the nation's current fascination with railroad trains, "underground road" became "underground railroad."

The Underground Railroad was the name given to a network of people, organizations, and places that emerged in the early 1800s to help runaway slaves escape from slavery. Whether Tice Davids' story is true or just a myth, it reflects the real stories of many fugitive slaves. Thousands received help on the Underground Railroad.

THE BEGINNING OF SLAVERY IN THE NEW LAND

The first Africans were brought to the Western Hemisphere to be slaves in the 1400s. European settlers and explorers brought them to the **colonies** to perform the difficult work of **cultivating** and taming the land. By the 1500s, thousands

Slaves harvest sugar cane in Antigua, an island in the Caribbean.

Slaves arrive at the Jamestown Colony in Virginia.

of people from Africa worked the mines and **plantations** in South America, Central America, and the Caribbean islands.

The first Africans brought to the colonies in America landed in Jamestown, Virginia, in 1619. At first, these Africans were treated like the **indentured servants** who came from Europe. Indentured servants were contracted to work for a period of time—usually seven years—in exchange for a boat ticket to the new land. After that period of time ended, these servants were granted their freedom. This kind of arrangement did not last long for the Africans in colonial America.

Slavery emerged gradually in the colonies. As the colonists bought houses, farming equipment and animals, they also bought slaves. All were legal property of the owner. Slave by slave, law by law, state by state, and year by year, the institution grew.

By 1790, there were nearly 700,000 slaves in the United

Slaves were considered "property" of the owner. They were bought and sold at public auctions like this one.

THE FIRST SLAVES

At first, Europeans tried to **enslave** the Native American Indian population. But American Indians did not make "good" slaves. Most of them died from the harsh treatment they received and from the diseases brought to the region by the Europeans. Others simply ran away.

Many southern plantations like this one would not have succeeded without the work of slaves.

States. Most toiled on plantations and farms in the South. By 1810, the number of slaves had increased to one million, and by 1830, to two million. By 1860, a year before the Civil War began, nearly four million African Americans were slaves in the United States.

RESISTANCE

From the beginning, African Americans resisted enslavement. Some planned and carried out **revolts**. In 1822, in Charleston, South Carolina, a former slave named Denmark Vesey planned a rebellion. However, his plan was discovered, and he and thirty-seven other African Americans were executed.

Another famous revolt was carried out by a slave in Virginia named Nat Turner. In 1831, Turner led a revolt that took the lives of more than sixty white men, women, and children. He and more than one hundred African Americans were killed as a result.

Some slaves killed themselves rather than be enslaved. Others chose to run away in hopes of reaching freedom in the North. Some slaves did find freedom. Many of those who did were helped by people who were opposed to slavery.

THE LIFE OF A SLAVE

Most slaves lived in cabins with dirt floors and no windows. The cabins had little or no furniture, and beds and pillows were made from straw. One set of clothing was usually given to each slave. Sometimes old shoes were provided, but many slaves went barefoot.

The majority of slaves worked in the fields, planting and harvesting crops. The average workday lasted twelve to fifteen hours. Men, women, and children toiled side by side.

A group of slaves stand outside their quarters on a plantation on Cockspur Island, Georgia.

9

OPPOSITION TO SLAVERY

Over time, growing numbers of people began to speak out against slavery. One of the first groups to do so was the Quakers. They were a religious group that was also known as the Society of Friends. The Quakers began an organized effort to **abolish** slavery as early as 1724.

Anthony Benezet, a Quaker, wrote this book called *Observations on the Inslaving, Importing and Purchasing of Negroes.* Benezet was one of many Quakers who was against slavery.

OBSERVATIONS

On the Inslaving, importing and purchasing of

Negroes;

With some Advice thereon, extracted from the Epistle of the Yearly-Meeting of the People called QUAKERS, held at *London* in the Year 1748.

Anthony Benezet

When ye spread forth your Hands, I will hide mine Eyes from you, yea when ye make many Prayers I will not hear; your Hands are full of Blood. Wash ye, make you clean, put away the Evil of your Doings from before mine Eyes Isai. 1, 15.

Is not this the Feast that I have chosen, to loose the Bands of Wickedness, to undo the heavy Burden, to let the Oppressed go free, and that ye break every Yoke, Chap. 58, 7.

Second Edition.

GERMANTOWN:
Printed by CHRISTOPHER SOWER. 1760.

Following the Revolutionary War (1775–1783), when the American colonies gained their independence from Britain, even more more people opposed slavery. Some American patriots, such as Patrick Henry, Benjamin Franklin, and Alexander Hamilton, felt that if the new nation were to live up to the ideals of freedom for which it had fought, then slavery had to be abolished.

Moved by the spirit of the Revolutionary War, states in the North began to abolish slavery. In 1777, Vermont was the first state to pass a law ending slavery. By the time New Jersey did the same in 1846, most Northern states had legally abolished slavery.

In the South, it was a different story. A few plantation owners freed their slaves as a reward for fighting in the Revolutionary War. In general, however, the South continued to

Although some slaves were forced to have multiple children, family members were often broken up and sold to different owners.

increase its supply of slaves. Landowners needed large numbers of slaves to work the abundant farmland there.

In 1807, the United States Congress passed a law to end African slave trade. This law made it more difficult to bring Africans to U.S. shores, but it did little to stop slavery. Other methods were used to increase the supply of slaves. Slaves were encouraged and often forced to have several children. As a result, the population of slaves continued to grow.

THE BEGINNING OF THE UNDERGROUND RAILROAD

From the beginning of slavery in America, slaves seeking freedom ran away. But there was no organized effort to assist **fugitive** slaves until after the Revolutionary War. In the 1800s, abolitionists became more outspoken in their campaign against slavery. Some abolitionists demanded an immediate end to the institution. At the same time, slaveholders grew more determined to defend the labor system on which they had built their economy.

In January 1831, *The Liberator* made its debut. It was a weekly newspaper published by abolitionist William Lloyd Garrison. In the first issue, Garrison wrote, "I will not equivocate—I will not excuse—I will not retreat a

By the 1830s, more people began to speak out openly against slavery. Here, abolitionist Wendell Phillips speaks in front of a crowd on Boston Common in Massachusetts.

12

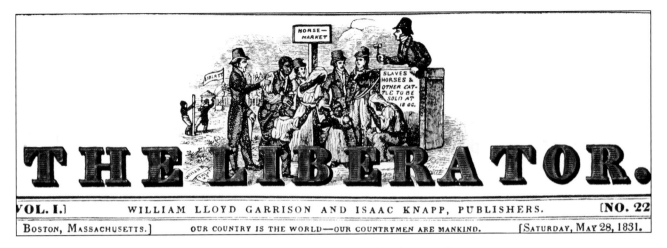

William Lloyd Garrison used his newspaper, *The Liberator*, to express his views on slavery.

single inch—AND I WILL BE HEARD." *The Liberator* became an important tool used to make the case for the abolition of slavery.

In 1833, Garrison and other antislavery supporters met in Philadelphia to organize the American Anti-Slavery Society. Soon, antislavery organizations sprang up in towns and cities throughout the North. They held public meetings. Often at these meetings, African Americans who had escaped slavery in the South told what it was like to be a slave. Some, such as Frederick Douglass, wrote books about their experiences. Soon, groups of people and organizations began working together to help fugitive slaves. These organized efforts became known as the "Underground Railroad."

Many abolitionists became workers on the Underground Railroad. They included women and men, African Americans and whites. Some people gave money to buy food and clothing for escaped slaves. They were called "agents." "Stationmasters" shared their homes, churches, and

13

Some southerners who opposed slavery helped fugitive slaves escape.

businesses (known as "stations") to provide safe havens for fugitives. "Conductors" helped to guide escaping slaves to safety. Escaping or fugitive slaves were called "packages," "freight," or "passengers."

Anyone who helped slaves to escape faced danger. White workers on the Underground Railroad who were caught in the South could be fined or sent to prison. The risks for African American conductors were even greater. They could be enslaved, whipped, or even killed if they were caught.

THE PASSENGERS

Those slaves who dared to attempt escape were gripped by fear that they would be caught. They had to travel hundreds of miles, often on foot, through woods, over fields, and across bodies of water. Under cover of darkness, runaways followed the North Star, which pointed the way north. On dark and stormy nights, escaping slaves felt for moss on nearby trees. They knew that moss grows on the north side of trees, helping them to find their way.

Sometimes escaping slaves were given refuge by free African Americans or by kind whites. Accepting help from anyone was extremely risky. A person thought to be a friend could actually be a supporter of slavery.

Escaping slaves were gripped by fear, knowing that they would be punished harshly if they were caught.

Some slaves were afraid to try running away. Here, a plantation schoolteacher offers to help a slave escape.

15

The Underground Railroad gave escaping slaves greater hope of reaching freedom. Escaping slaves could find food and a place to rest at stations along the way. Stationmasters would direct them to the next station. Often, a sign or marker, such as a lantern placed on a special post, identified a station.

In the early days of the Underground Railroad, most fugitives were men. Women did not want to leave family members behind, especially their children. But as more slaves became aware of the help they could receive on the Underground Railroad, women and children gained the courage to attempt their escapes. Sometimes entire families escaped together. Wagons were often used to transport them.

This painting by Charles Webber, created in 1893, depicts a family in Ohio helping runaway slaves.

Josiah Henson's life story is believed to have inspired Harriet Beecher Stowe's book *Uncle Tom's Cabin*, about the life of a slave.

SONGS WITH HIDDEN MEANING

Fugitive slaves sometimes sang songs to communicate with one another on the Underground Railroad. Many songs had hidden meanings. "Follow the Drinking Gourd" was one such song used on the Underground Railroad.

When the sun comes back and the first quail calls,
Follow the drinking gourd.
For the old man is a-waiting to carry you to freedom
If you follow the drinking gourd.

"When the sun comes back" refers to winter and spring, when the altitude of the sun at noon appears to be higher each day. Quails are migratory birds that spend the winter in the South. The drinking gourd is another name for a constellation, or cluster of stars, called the Big Dipper. Finally, the old man is Peg Leg Joe, who, some historians believe, traveled the South teaching the song to slaves. The song tells slaves to escape in the winter and to walk toward the Big Dipper. Eventually, they will meet a guide who will help them.

Underground Railroad agents would simply cover the fugitive slaves in the wagon with blankets, hay, or vegetables. Sometimes, secret compartments were built in which slaves could lie hidden and covered.

No matter how a slave traveled, the trip was always dangerous. In Kentucky, a slave named Josiah Henson decided to run away to Canada with his wife and four children. In 1830, he carried his two youngest children in a knapsack on his back. After several nights of travel, the family reached the Ohio River and crossed into Indiana.

Fugitive slaves from the South are led onboard a Mississippi steamboat.

Several weeks later, they arrived in Cincinnati, Ohio. There they were befriended by a tribe of American Indians who gave them food and shelter. In Sandusky, Ohio, a Scottish steamboat captain gave them passage to Buffalo, New York. From Buffalo, the family made its way to Canada and, finally, to freedom.

For six weeks, the Hensons had endured hunger, made their way across rugged terrain, fought off wild animals, and avoided slave catchers to make their escape. Once in Canada, Henson sought to help other slaves secure their freedom. He even made a trip into Kentucky, where he had once been a slave, to guide a group of escaping slaves to Canada.

Henry Brown found a clever way to escape from slavery in Richmond, Virginia. He decided to ship himself to Philadelphia, Pennsylvania, in a box. On top of the box, written in large letters, were the words "This side up with care." With only a small container of water and a few biscuits, Brown began his trip to Philadelphia. He also brought along a tool so he could bore small holes in the box through which he could get fresh air. Twenty-six hours later, Brown arrived in Philadelphia. He then moved to Boston, where he became an abolitionist speaker and was active in the Underground Railroad.

Other escapes involved careful disguises. William and Ellen Craft were married. But they were owned by different masters, so they lived on different plantations in Macon, Georgia. Ellen worked in the house of the master. William,

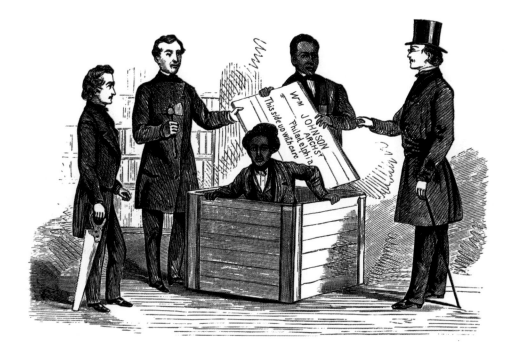

Henry Brown shipped himself in a crate from Virginia to Pennsylvania. He arrived in Philadelphia tired and bruised, but free.

19

This illustration shows a view of the State House in Philadelphia in the early 1800s. Philadelphia was known as a city where runaway slaves could find help.

a cabinetmaker, was allowed to do work outside of the plantation when his responsibilities there were finished. He saved the money he earned. In 1848, the Crafts decided to make their escape.

Ellen was so light-skinned that she could pass for white. The couple's plan was to disguise Ellen as a sickly white man traveling to Philadelphia to receive medical treatment with William, who played the role of the faithful slave. Ellen dressed in men's clothing and wore a bandage around her face, pretending to have a toothache. The Crafts traveled by train and steamboat through South Carolina, North Carolina, Virginia, Maryland, and Washington, D.C. They arrived in Philadelphia on Christmas Day in 1848. During their bold and daring escape to freedom, they fooled hundreds of people.

Philadelphia was not always a safe place for escaped slaves. Slave catchers lurked everywhere. So the Crafts moved to Boston, Massachusetts. When the federal government passed a new Fugitive Slave Law in 1850 that permitted fugitive slaves to be captured anywhere in the United States, the Crafts moved to England.

There were countless escape stories told by members of the Underground Railroad. It is estimated that between 50,000 and 100,000 slaves were helped by this network. Some of the slaves who found freedom in the North and in Canada wrote about their escapes and their lives in bondage. The books were called slave narratives. These slave narratives provided important information about the Underground Railroad.

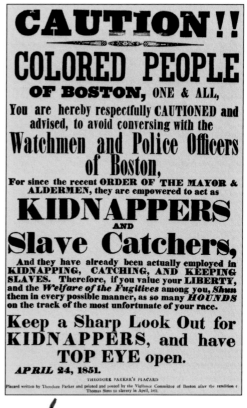

This poster warns African Americans in Boston to watch out for slave catchers. Only a few days earlier, a fugitive slave named Thomas Sims was arrested in Boston and returned to his owner in Georgia.

REWARD!

Slave catchers were men who earned money by catching fugitive slaves and returning them to their masters. Capturing runaway slaves could be very profitable. One slaveholder offered $500 each for two slaves who had escaped from his plantation. Most slave catchers were willing to use any method necessary to catch fugitive slaves. Some even captured free African Americans, took them to the South, and sold them into slavery.

Reward money was commonly offered to anyone who could catch a runaway slave.

STATIONS AND STATIONMASTERS

Stations and their stationmasters were crucial to the Underground Railroad. Finding a station often determined whether or not a slave escaped successfully. There were many different kinds of Underground Railroad stations. These included barns, hidden tunnels, attics, cellars, and secret rooms and closets in homes, churches, and businesses.

The Tallman House in Janesville, Wisconsin, was built especially to hide fugitive slaves. The twenty-room home had hiding places in both the attic and the basement and a lookout post on the roof. A secret stairway in a maid's closet

Homes along the Underground Railroad often had secret hideaways for slaves. What seems to be an ordinary cupboard on the left actually contains a small space where slaves could safely rest out of sight.

led to an underground tunnel. At the end of tunnel was the Rock River, where fugitives were taken by riverboat to the town of Milton, Wisconsin.

The Stage Coach Inn in Milton was also an Underground Railroad station. A tunnel connected the inn to a cabin nearby. Fugitive slaves were taken to the cabin. In case of danger, they could enter the tunnel through a trapdoor in the cabin and find safety in a hiding place in the inn.

Perhaps the most recognized station on the Underground Railroad was the home of Levi and Catherine Coffin in Newport, Indiana. Levi Coffin was born in North Carolina. A Quaker who opposed slavery, he tried to start a school for

★ ★ ★ ★

slaves, but their owners refused to allow the slaves to attend. In 1824, he married Catherine White. The couple moved to Newport in 1826.

Newport was located on the eastern end of the Ohio River above Cincinnati, Ohio. Ohio was a free state, and Cincinnati was one of the cities that fugitive slaves often passed through on their way north. Soon after arriving in Newport, Coffin learned that a route on the Underground Railroad passed near his area. Fugitive slaves sought refuge in a nearby community of free African Americans. Many of the fugitive slaves were captured, however, because the African American community was often the first place slave catchers would search.

Levi Coffin and his wife helped more than 3,000 fugitive slaves to safety.

Coffin and his wife decided to act. They opened the doors of their home to escaping slaves. Word traveled quickly to African American communities and to abolitionists. From 1827 to 1847, fugitive slaves made their way to the Coffins' two-story, eight-room brick house. Over time, three different lines on the Underground Railroad

Coffin House

came together at the Coffin house. Levi Coffin became known as the "president" of the Underground Railroad.

Thomas Garrett was another stationmaster on the Underground Railroad. Born in Pennsylvania, Garrett settled in Wilmington, Delaware, in 1822. He began helping runaway slaves at his home, offering them food and shelter.

In 1848, Garrett was arrested for helping a fugitive slave family travel from Wilmington to Philadelphia. He was convicted of breaking the Fugitive Slave Law and fined $5,000.

25

Many homes that were part of the Underground Railroad, such as the Johnson House shown here, are today National Historic Landmarks. The Johnson family aided many slaves from their home in Philadelphia.

He did not have enough money to pay the fine, so he was forced to sell his belongings at a public auction. It is estimated that more than two thousand fugitive slaves passed through his home.

Many stationmasters were African Americans. Some were born free in the North. Others had escaped from slavery in the South and settled in northern cities.

Jermain Wesley Loguen was called the "Underground Railroad King." After escaping from slavery in Tennessee, he settled in Syracuse, New York, and became a minister.

Loguen and his wife Caroline established Underground Railroad stations at their home and at the church where Loguen served as pastor. More than fifteen hundred fugitive slaves reached Canada through the help of the Loguens.

Another well-known stationmaster and abolitionist was Frederick Douglass. After escaping from slavery in Maryland when he was twenty years old, Douglass became involved in the antislavery cause. He traveled throughout the North speaking about slavery and published a newspaper called *North Star*.

Frederick Douglass was a leader of the abolitionist movement. He was a brilliant public speaker, and gave moving speeches in support of ending slavery.

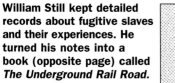

William Still kept detailed records about fugitive slaves and their experiences. He turned his notes into a book (opposite page) called *The Underground Rail Road*.

When he moved to Rochester, New York, his home became a station on the Underground Railroad. Douglass was not a full-time stationmaster because of his many other activities in support of the abolitionist movement. Still, many fugitive slaves found shelter in his home on their way to Canada.

* * * *

William Still was born in New Jersey in 1821. In 1844, he moved to Philadelphia, Pennsylvania, and married. He joined an abolitionist group, and in 1847, the Philadelphia Society for the Abolition of Slavery hired him as a clerk. In this position, he spent many years helping fugitive slaves who passed through Philadelphia.

At first, he kept notes. Then, in 1851, he began writing down the names and stories of those fugitive slaves being helped by the abolitionist group. After slavery was abolished, Still published this information. *The Underground Rail Road*, released in 1872, provided detailed accounts of the Railroad and the fugitive slaves who were helped by it.

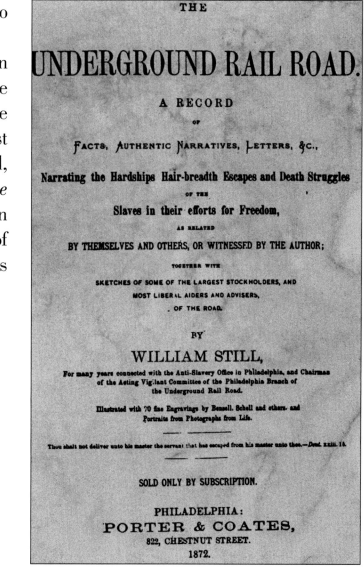

BROTHERLY LOVE

One of the fugitive slaves William Still assisted on the Underground Railroad was his brother, Peter. When Still's mother escaped from slavery in Maryland many years before, she had to leave behind her two young sons, Peter and Leven. Both were sold in the South and ended up working on a plantation in Alabama. Leven died, but Peter escaped and eventually met his brother William in Philadelphia.

Conductors on the
Underground Railroad
direct runaway slaves
to safety.

THE CONDUCTORS

Usually, conductors on the Underground Railroad were thought to be people who traveled to the South to lead slaves to freedom. A number of conductors, such as Harriet Tubman, did just that. But a conductor could also be a driver who took a wagonload of slaves to the next station. It could be a steamship worker who hid slaves as stowaways. It could also be someone who went to the South to spread the word to slaves about the Underground Railroad and to offer them directions.

The conductor's job was the most dangerous one on the Underground Railroad. Conductors faced fines, imprisonment, and even death if they were caught. Like stationmasters, conductors were both white and African American. They were women and men.

Calvin Fairbank made his first trip to the South to help free slaves in 1837. He had come to hate slavery while he was a student at Oberlin College in Ohio. In 1844, he and a

Calvin Fairbank was put in prison for aiding a runaway slave.

Harriet Tubman was so successful in escorting escaping slaves that slave owners offered as much as $40,000 for her capture.

schoolteacher from Vermont named Delia Webster were arrested for aiding in the escape of a slave. Webster was released and allowed to return to Vermont. Fairbank served several years in prison. After his release, he again became a conductor on the Underground Railroad.

The most famous conductor on the Underground Railroad was Harriet Tubman. She earned the name "Moses" because of her exploits leading slaves out of the South. Tubman was born into slavery, but escaped in 1849 to Philadelphia, where she met William Still. A short time later, she returned to the South to lead her sister and her sister's children out of slavery.

Between 1851 and 1860, Tubman made numerous trips to the South to guide slaves to the North and Canada. Tubman once boasted that she had never lost a passenger.

LIBERTY OR DEATH

"I had reasoned this out in my mind; there was one thing of two things I had a right to, liberty or death: If I could not have one, I would have the other; for no man should take me alive."

—Harriet Tubman

This photograph shows Tubman (far left) with some of the people she helped to rescue from slavery.

No one really knows the exact number of slaves she guided to freedom. Estimates range from seventy-five to three hundred. Whatever the total, Harriet Tubman's name is forever etched in history because of her courage, determination, and commitment.

ESCAPE ROUTES

During the early years of the Underground Railroad, most fugitive slaves came from states such as Kentucky, Maryland, and Virginia. These states were located close to free states in the North.

Escaping from states in the Deep South was extremely difficult and took a much longer period of time. Some slaves who did escape from states in the Deep South hid in big

Many slaves escaped along the Mississippi River or the Appalachian Mountains. Sometimes the trip could be made in a couple of months; for others it took up to a year.

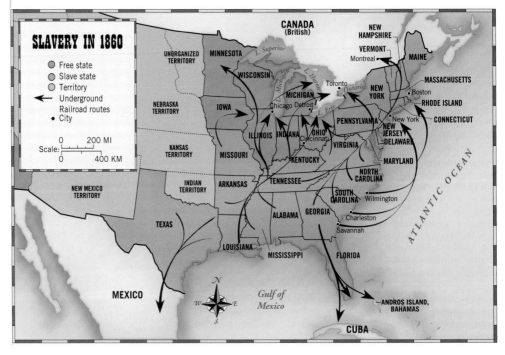

This illustration shows a group of slaves escaping under cover of night.

cities in the South or found refuge with American Indians. Some went to Mexico, while others established communities in the swamps of North Carolina, the bayous of Louisiana, and the mountains of Tennessee and Kentucky. But as the Underground Railroad network expanded, more slaves from the Deep South fled to the North.

Many slaves learned about the Underground Railroad from conductors. Underground Railroad routes ran across rivers and valleys, over mountains, and into small towns and big cities. Usually, Railroad stations were about 10 to 20 miles (16 to 32 kilometers) apart. The average distance between them was about twelve miles (19 km). That was the distance a wagon could cover in one night or that a person could travel on foot in about twelve hours.

★　★　★　★

BEYOND THE LAW

The Fugitive Slave Act of 1793 gave slave owners the right to recapture their runaway slaves, but many fugitives still settled in cities and towns in the North. Officials in many northern areas did not enforce the law. In some cities, when the law was enforced, people opposed to slavery prevented fugitive slaves from being taken back into slavery.

Supporters of slavery were always on the lookout for information about fugitive slaves, so Underground Railroad routes had to be kept secret. Because of this need for secrecy, many routes are now lost to history. But in his book *The Underground Railroad: From Slavery to Freedom*, Wilbur Siebert included a map of escape routes. The routes run through Missouri, Kentucky, West Virginia, Pennsylvania, New York, New Jersey, Delaware, Ohio, Illinois, Michigan, and the New England states.

FREEDOM LAND

In some areas of the North, African American communities readily accepted their "brothers and sisters." Some fugitive slaves found work in the North, started families, and became important participants in the antislavery movement. After escaping from slavery in Maryland, Frederick Douglass made his home in Massachusetts. He later moved to Rochester, New York, where he continued to carry out his antislavery activities. Other fugitives settled in cities such as New York, Philadelphia, Hartford, New Haven, Boston, and Detroit.

But as more and more slaves escaped to freedom, slave owners became more determined to reclaim their valuable property. More slave catchers became active in the business of capturing runaway slaves. As a result, Canada became the destination for many fugitives.

The Fugitive Slave Law made it dangerous for slaves to stay in the northern states. Many continued on to Canada, including Montreal, shown here.

The Canadian government had no fugitive slave laws. African American men were even given the right to vote. Toronto, Niagara Falls, Hamilton, and Windsor were a few of the cities in which fugitive slaves settled. Some of these newly free African Americans formed their own towns and established their own schools, businesses,

This school in Ontario was part of a village for fugitive slaves. Shown here is the class of 1909, which included both black and white children.

and churches. Others **integrated** into white communities. The number of fugitive slaves who settled in Canada is not known. But for thousands, the country north of the border was the land of freedom.

THE END OF SLAVERY AND THE UNDERGROUND RAILROAD

By the 1850s, differences between the North and South had reached a crisis. As the North turned from an agricultural economy to a manufacturing one, the need for slave labor waned. The northern states had long abolished slavery, and they were against slavery spreading into the country's new territories and states. In the South, however, a booming agricultural economy emerged. Many Southerners depended more and more on free slave labor.

In 1860, the issue of slavery was one of many that divided North and South. On April 12, 1861, the war

African American guards of the 107th United States Colored Troops pose outside a guardhouse in Virginia. By the end of the Civil War, about 179,000 black men served as soldiers in the U.S. Army.

between the North and South, called the Civil War, began. It would last until April 1865.

The Underground Railroad continued to operate as best as it could during the war. Many agents and conductors assisted the Union army in various ways. Harriet Tubman acted as a spy and a nurse. Frederick Douglass lobbied the government to allow African Americans to fight. This became a reality in 1862, when Congress passed an act that permitted African Americans to fight as soldiers in defense of the Union.

After four long, grueling years, the Civil War ended. The North was victorious, and the Union was saved. But slavery in the United States did not legally end until the Thirteenth **Amendment** to the United States Constitution was **ratified** in December 1865. Finally, the institution that kept millions of African Americans in bondage, divided the country, and had caused so many deaths was abolished.

With its end came the end of the Underground Railroad. Agents were no longer needed to supply money for food and clothing for fugitive slaves. Stationmasters were no longer needed to provide shelter and protection. Conductors no longer had to guide escaping slaves to freedom.

After the war, a book about Harriet Tubman was published. William Still published *The Underground Rail Road*. Levi Coffin's **autobiography** was published. These and other publications brought the good deeds of the Underground Railroad to the public. Even today, historic sites and museums continue to spotlight the courageous men and women who carried out the important work of the Underground Railroad.

A group of freed slaves gather on a plantation in Hilton Head, South Carolina, during the Civil War.

Glossary

abolish—to end something, such as slavery

abolitionist—one who supports the end of something, such as slavery

amendment—change made to the U.S. Constitution in a bill or law

autobiography—a person's life story, written by himself or herself

colony—settlement of people living in a land outside their home country, but under the power of the home country

cultivate—prepare for crops

enslave—make a slave of

fugitive—runaway slave

indentured servant—person who worked for a specific
number of years in exchange for travel expenses

integrated—combined or joined together as one

plantation—large farm in the Caribbean and later in the
Southern states that grew cash crops and was
worked by African American slaves

ratified—approved

revolt—an organized conflict

Timeline: The Undergound

1619	1775	1831	1838	1847
	The first abolitionist group in the United States is founded in Philadelphia.	The term "Underground Railroad" comes into use. The American Anti-Slavery Society is founded in Philadelphia.	Frederick Douglass escapes from slavery.	The first issue of *North Star*, an abolitionist newspaper begun by Frederick Douglass, is published.
The first African slaves brought to the United States arrive in Virginia.				

Railroad

Harriet Tubman escapes from slavery.

The Fugitive Slave Act is passed, providing for the return of runaway slaves to their owners.

In 1852, *Uncle Tom's Cabin*, written by Harriet Beecher Stowe, is published.

Harriet Tubman makes her first trip back to the South to help other slaves escape to freedom on the Underground Railroad.

The war between the North and the South, called the American Civil War, begins.

On January 1, President Abraham Lincoln signs the Emancipation Proclamation, freeing all the slaves in the states of the Confederacy.

The Civil War ends. Victory by the North preserves the Union. The Thirteenth Amendment is approved, abolishing slavery in the United States.

45

To Find Out More

BOOKS AND VIDEOS

Bial, Raymond. *The Underground Railroad*. Turtleback Books, reissued 1999.

Hamilton, Virginia. *Many Thousand Gone: African Americans from Slavery to Freedom*. New York: Random House, 1995.

Haskins, Jim. *Get On Board: The Story of the Underground Railroad.* Scholastic, reissued 1997.

Perrin, Pat. *The Underground Railroad: Life on the Road to Freedom*. Discovery Enterprises Ltd., 1999.

ONLINE SITES

HistoryChannel.com—The Underground Railroad
http://www.historychannel.com/exhibits/undergroundrr/people.html

National Geographic Underground Railroad Site
http://www.nationalgeographic.com/railroad/

National Park Service—Learn About the Underground Railroad
http://209.10.16.21/template/Frontend/learn.CFM

Index

Bold numbers indicate illustrations.

About the Author

Wade Hudson is the author of many books for young people. He compiled *Pass It On: African-American Poetry for Children* published by Scholastic. He is the author of three Great Black Heroes books: *Five Brave Explorers*, *Five Notable Inventors*, and *Five Bold Freedom Fighters*, all published by Scholastic. His most recent book is the Scholastic title *Powerful Words: More Than 200 Years of Extraordinary Writing by African Americans*. Mr. Hudson and his wife Cheryl are the force behind Just Us Books, which has been publishing children's books that reflect the African American experience since 1988.